HOW TO LIVE WITH
AN ADHD
HUSBAND

Overcoming Challenges and the
Effects of ADHD on Your Marriage

DR. MICHEAL WILSON

"Life isn't about waiting for the storm to pass... it's about learning to dance in the rain!"
— Vivian Greene

HOW TO LIVE WITH AN
ADHD HUSBAND

OVERCOMING CHALLENGES AND THE EFFECTS
OF ADHD ON YOUR MARRIAGE

Bonus:
20 ADHD-
friendly
activities for
couples

DR. MICHEAL WILSON

Contents

Introduction

I've been a therapist for over 20 years, and I've worked with many couples where one partner has ADHD. I've seen firsthand the challenges that these couples face, but I've also seen the incredible love and resilience that can exist in these relationships. I know that living with an ADHD husband can be challenging. You may feel like you're constantly picking up after him, or that you're the only one who can keep track of anything. You may feel frustrated, angry, or even resentful.

But I also know that it's possible to have a happy and fulfilling relationship with an ADHD husband. It takes work, but it's worth it. In this book, I'm going to share with you the things that I've learned from working with couples with ADHD. I'm going to give you practical tips on how to manage your husband's symptoms, how to communicate effectively, and how to build a strong and loving relationship.

I'm also going to share some stories from my practice. These stories will show you that you're not alone and that it's possible to overcome the challenges of living with an ADHD husband. So if you're feeling overwhelmed, or if you're just looking for some support, I encourage you to read on. This book is for you.

I remember one couple that I worked with, let's call them Jeff and Mary. Jeff had ADHD, and Mary was struggling to cope with his symptoms. She felt like she was constantly picking up after him, and she was starting to feel resentful.

I worked with Jeff and Mary to develop a plan to manage his symptoms. We talked about setting up a routine, using reminders, and finding ways to reduce distractions. We also talked about communication, and how to express their feelings healthily. Over time, Jeff and Mary made some significant progress. They were able to develop a better understanding of each other's needs, and they were able to communicate more effectively. They also found ways to work together to manage Jeff's symptoms.

As a result of their hard work, Jeff and Mary were able to build a stronger and more loving relationship. They were able to overcome the challenges of living with ADHD, and they were able to create a happy and fulfilling life together.

The journey isn't quick or easy, but so worth it. A peaceful, loving relationship is possible. In the following chapters, I will walk you through the techniques and interventions that have helped hundreds of couples thrive together in the face of ADHD struggles. Take heart that positive change lies ahead.

Life with an ADHD husband is an exhilarating rollercoaster ride—one filled with boundless energy, creativity, and unexpected twists. Yet, amidst the whirlwind of emotions, challenges, and joys, lies a unique journey that can be both fulfilling and overwhelming. This book is your compass, your guide to navigating the uncharted waters of living with an extraordinary partner, as you embark on a transformative voyage of love, understanding, and growth.

In "How to live with an ADHD husband," we delve deep into the heart of relationships, exploring the intricacies of loving someone with ADHD. With empathy and expertise, this book unveils the captivating dynamics that lie within these partnerships, revealing the hidden gems that make them truly special.

Through personal stories, expert insights, and practical strategies, we unravel the mysteries of ADHD, shedding light on the fascinating ways an ADHD brain works and how it shapes the very essence of your relationship. You will discover that beyond the initial challenges lies a world brimming with untapped potential, where creativity and spontaneity thrive, and where love blossoms in the most unexpected places.

Understanding and supporting your ADHD husband can be a fulfilling journey of self-discovery, as you learn to embrace the quirks, unlock the strengths, and navigate the complexities of your unique bond. With patience and open hearts, you'll forge a connection that transcends any obstacle, weathering storms and celebrating triumphs together.

This book is not just a guide; it's an invitation to embrace the adventure of living with an ADHD husband—to embark on a quest that empowers both of you to become the best version of yourselves. You'll find invaluable tools to communicate effectively, manage challenges with grace, and nurture the profound love that sets your relationship apart.

As you delve into these pages, you'll find solace in knowing that you're not alone on this journey. Many others have walked the path before you, and their experiences have paved the way for you to embrace this beautiful adventure wholeheartedly.

So, fasten your seatbelts, open your hearts, and let "How to live with an ADHD husband" be your guiding light to a more profound and fulfilling love, enriched by the vibrant hues of ADHD's extraordinary world. Together, let's soar to new heights and unlock the extraordinary possibilities that await you in this captivating voyage of love and understanding.

"When you have exhausted all possibilities, remember this: you haven't." - Thomas Edison

Chapter One

Understanding ADHD

ADHD is a neurodevelopmental condition that affects both children and adults. It is characterized by persistent patterns of inattention, hyperactivity, and impulsivity that can significantly impact various aspects of an individual's life, including academic performance, work productivity, and personal relationships. This chapter aims to provide an in-depth understanding of ADHD, exploring its definition, prevalence, and the common symptoms experienced by adults with this condition.

What is ADHD?

ADHD is a complex and multifaceted condition that affects the brain's executive functions, which are responsible for regulating behaviors, emotions, and cognitive processes. While the exact cause of ADHD is not fully understood, research suggests that genetic and environmental factors play a significant role in its development.

It is estimated that ADHD affects around 9.4% of children and 4.4% of adults worldwide. However, many adults remain undiagnosed and untreated. Men are more likely than women to experience ADHD. There is believed to be a genetic component as ADHD tends to run in families, however environmental influences like brain injury or prenatal alcohol/drug exposure may also contribute to ADHD risk.

There are three primary subtypes of ADHD:

1. Predominantly Inattentive Presentation: Individuals with this subtype primarily struggle with attention and focus. They often have difficulty sustaining attention to tasks, following through on instructions, and organizing activities.

2. Predominantly Hyperactive-Impulsive Presentation: This subtype is distinguished by hyperactivity and impulsivity. This type of ADHD can cause a person to fidget or squirm, interrupt others, and have trouble waiting their turn.

3. Combined Presentation: As the name implies, this subtype exhibits a combination of inattentive and hyperactive-impulsive symptoms.

Common Symptoms of ADHD in Adults

Inattention Symptoms:

1. Difficulty sustaining focus: Adults with ADHD often find it hard to maintain attention on tasks that are repetitive, mundane, or require prolonged mental effort. As a result, they may frequently switch between activities or become easily distracted by external stimuli.

2. Poor organization and time management: Adults with ADHD may struggle to manage time effectively, leading to difficulties in meeting deadlines or maintaining a consistent daily routine. They might misplace items, forget appointments, and have a disorganized living or working space.

3. Forgetfulness: Frequent memory lapses, such as forgetting important dates, names, or tasks, are common among adults with ADHD. This forgetfulness can lead to frustration and can affect personal and professional relationships.

4. Difficulty following through on tasks: Adults with ADHD may have difficulty completing projects or fulfilling responsibilities, even if they are capable of starting them. This challenge often stems from difficulties with maintaining focus and sustained effort.

5. Avoidance of tasks requiring sustained mental effort: Tasks that demand prolonged concentration, such as reading lengthy documents or engaging in detailed planning, can be particularly challenging for adults with ADHD, leading to procrastination and avoidance.

Hyperactivity and Impulsivity Symptoms:

1. Restlessness and fidgeting: Unlike the physical hyperactivity often observed in children, adults with ADHD may experience inner restlessness, feeling as if they are "on the go" mentally. They may fidget or engage in repetitive movements to cope with this restlessness.

2. Impulsive decision-making: Adults with ADHD may act impulsively, making decisions without fully considering the consequences. This impulsivity can lead to financial difficulties, relationship conflicts, and risky behaviors.

3. Difficulty waiting or taking turns: Impulsivity can manifest in social situations, where adults with ADHD may interrupt conversations, have difficulty waiting for their turn, or exhibit impatience.

4. Excessive talking: Adults with ADHD may struggle to control the volume or amount of speech, often speaking rapidly and excessively, which can be perceived as disruptive in certain situations.

5. Risk-taking behavior: Some adults with ADHD may engage in risky behaviors without fully evaluating potential dangers. These behaviors can include reckless driving, substance abuse, and other thrill-seeking activities.

It's essential to recognize that everyone can experience occasional symptoms of inattention, hyperactivity, or impulsivity. However, for individuals with ADHD, these symptoms are persistent, severe, and interfere with daily functioning. If you suspect that you or someone you know may have ADHD, it is crucial to seek professional evaluation and diagnosis from a qualified healthcare professional or mental health specialist.

The Impact of ADHD on Relationships

Attention-Deficit/Hyperactivity Disorder (ADHD) not only affects the individual diagnosed with the condition but also has a profound impact on their relationships with family members, friends, and romantic partners. The symptoms of ADHD, which include inattention, impulsivity, and hyperactivity, can lead to misunderstandings, frustrations, and challenges in maintaining healthy and satisfying relationships. Understanding and addressing the impact of ADHD on relationships is crucial for fostering understanding, empathy, and effective communication.

1. Communication Challenges: Individuals with ADHD may have difficulty paying attention and listening actively during conversations. They may become easily distracted, interrupt others, or struggle to remember important details. As a result, their partners or loved ones might feel ignored or undervalued, leading to feelings of frustration and resentment.

2. Time Management and Organization: ADHD can affect an individual's ability to manage time effectively and maintain organization in daily tasks. This can lead to missed appointments, forgotten commitments, and a general sense of chaos in the relationship. Non-ADHD partners may feel burdened with managing responsibilities or perceive their partner as irresponsible.

3. Emotional Regulation: People with ADHD may experience difficulties in managing their emotions, leading to impulsive outbursts or emotional sensitivity. These emotional fluctuations can be challenging for their partners to navigate and understand, impacting the overall emotional climate of the relationship.

4. Division of Labor: The impact of ADHD on executive functions, such as planning and organizing, can affect the division of labor in a relationship. The non-ADHD partner might take on a disproportionate share of household responsibilities, leading to feelings of inequality and strain.

5. Intimacy and Affection: ADHD can also influence intimacy in relationships. The hyperactivity and impulsivity associated with ADHD may lead to impulsive actions that impact emotional and physical intimacy. Additionally, untreated symptoms might result in distraction and decreased interest in maintaining emotional connections.

6. Conflict and Frustration: Communication difficulties, emotional regulation challenges, and time management issues can all contribute to increased conflict in relationships involving someone with ADHD. Conflicts may arise from misunderstandings or the feeling of not being heard or supported.

Despite these challenges, it is essential to remember that ADHD is a manageable condition, and with understanding, support, and treatment, individuals with ADHD and their partners can develop strategies to navigate these difficulties together. Open and honest communication, seeking professional guidance, and learning coping techniques can significantly improve the quality of relationships impacted by ADHD.

Moreover, involving both partners in the treatment process can lead to better cooperation, empathy, and shared responsibility in managing the condition's impact on their relationship. By working together as a team, couples can build stronger, more resilient bonds and create an environment that fosters love, support, and understanding for both partners involved.

Chapter Two

Communicating Effectively with Your ADHD Husband

Any healthy relationship is built on effective communication. When one partner has ADHD, communication dynamics may face special difficulties. In this chapter, we'll look at ways to have a productive conversation with your ADHD husband while emphasizing active listening skills and clear expectations.

Active Listening Techniques

Active listening is a fundamental aspect of effective communication that involves giving your full attention to the speaker and demonstrating understanding and empathy. When communicating with your ADHD husband, employing active listening techniques can help foster a deeper connection and ensure that both partners feel heard and valued.

a. Maintain Eye Contact: Establishing eye contact while your husband is speaking shows that you are fully engaged in the conversation and interested in what he has to say. This simple gesture can enhance the sense of connection during communication.

b. Minimize Distractions: Creating a distraction-free environment during conversations can help your husband focus and express his thoughts more effectively. Turn off electronic devices, find a quiet space, and eliminate any potential interruptions.

c. Practice Reflective Listening: Reflective listening involves paraphrasing what your husband has said to ensure that you understand his message accurately. This technique helps clarify any potential misunderstandings and demonstrates that you are actively trying to comprehend his perspective.

d. Validate His Feelings: Show empathy and understanding by acknowledging your husband's emotions and validating his experiences. Let him know that you understand how he feels and that his feelings are important to you.

e. Be Patient: People with ADHD may take longer to express their thoughts or may struggle with verbalizing their feelings. Be patient and allow your husband the time he needs to communicate comfortably.

f. Avoid Interrupting: Interrupting during conversations can be particularly challenging for individuals with ADHD, as it can disrupt their train of thought. Practice patience and avoid interrupting to create a supportive environment for communication.

Setting Clear Expectations

ADHD can lead to difficulties with time management, organization, and follow-through. Setting clear expectations can help your husband better understand what is required of him and reduce misunderstandings and frustrations.

a. Use Clear and Direct Language: When communicating expectations, use straightforward and unambiguous language. Avoid using vague terms and be specific about what you expect from your husband.

b. Prioritize Key Information: People with ADHD may struggle with information overload. Highlight the most critical points and repeat them if necessary to ensure that your husband grasps the essential details.

c. Break Tasks into Smaller Steps: Large tasks can feel overwhelming for individuals with ADHD.

Breaking tasks into smaller, manageable steps can make them more approachable and increase the likelihood of successful completion.

d. Use Visual Aids and Reminders: Visual aids, such as checklists, calendars, and reminder notes, can be helpful tools for individuals with ADHD to stay organized and remember important tasks or events.

e. Set Realistic Goals: Setting achievable goals ensures that your husband can meet expectations without feeling overwhelmed. Celebrate his accomplishments, no matter how small, to encourage continued progress.

f. Encourage Open Communication: Create a safe and non-judgmental space for your husband to communicate openly about his struggles and challenges. Encouraging open communication fosters trust and allows for collaborative problem-solving.

g. Recognize Effort: Acknowledge your husband's efforts in meeting expectations and managing his ADHD symptoms. Positive reinforcement can be a powerful motivator and can boost his self-esteem.

Strategies for Handling Misunderstandings

Handling misunderstandings with an ADHD husband requires patience, empathy, and effective communication. ADHD can impact a person's ability to focus, listen, and process information, which may lead to more frequent misunderstandings in the relationship. Here are some strategies to navigate misunderstandings and maintain a strong connection with your ADHD husband:

1. Educate Yourself about ADHD: Understanding ADHD and its effects on communication and behavior is crucial for handling misunderstandings effectively. Educate yourself about the symptoms and challenges associated with ADHD, which can help you approach the situation with empathy and compassion.

2. Choose the Right Time and Setting: Timing and environment matter when addressing misunderstandings. Choose a calm and private setting to discuss any issues, and avoid confrontations when either of you is stressed or distracted.

3. Use Active Listening Techniques: Active listening is essential when communicating with an ADHD spouse. Give your husband your full attention, maintain eye contact, and use reflective listening to ensure you understand his perspective accurately.

4. Be Patient and Empathetic: Patience is a key virtue in handling misunderstandings with an ADHD husband. Understand that he may need extra time to process information and express himself. Show empathy and acknowledge the challenges he faces due to ADHD.

5. Practice Non-Verbal Communication: Non-verbal cues, such as body language and tone of voice, play a significant role in communication. Be mindful of your non-verbal signals and encourage your husband to do the same. Avoid negative body language that may be interpreted as judgmental or dismissive.

6. Use Clear and Direct Language: Be clear and concise when expressing your thoughts and feelings. Avoid vague or ambiguous language that might lead to further misunderstandings.

7. Break Down Complex Issues: When discussing complicated topics, break them down into smaller, more manageable parts. This approach can make it easier for your husband to process and respond effectively.

8. Provide Visual Aids and Reminders: Visual aids like charts, checklists, and calendars can be valuable tools for both of you to stay organized and keep track of important information or tasks.

9. Avoid Blame and Accusations: Giving your husband the finger or criticizing him over misunderstandings will make him defensive and escalate arguments. Instead, concentrate on teamwork and jointly coming up with answers.

Chapter Three

Building a Supportive Environment

Living with an ADHD husband can present unique challenges, but creating a supportive environment can significantly improve daily life for both partners. In this chapter, we will explore practical strategies for organizing the home to enhance focus and productivity, as well as the importance of establishing routines and schedules to promote stability and reduce stress.

Organizing the Home for Better Focus

A cluttered and disorganized home can exacerbate the symptoms of ADHD and make it difficult for your husband to stay focused and calm. Implementing organizational strategies can help create a more structured and supportive environment.

a. Declutter Regularly: Regularly decluttering and organizing the living spaces can reduce distractions and create a more visually calming environment. Encourage your husband to participate in this process to foster a sense of ownership and responsibility.

b. Create Designated Spaces: Designate specific areas for different activities, such as work, relaxation, and hobbies. Having dedicated spaces can help your husband mentally shift gears when needed and maintain better focus on tasks.

c. Use Visual Cues: Visual cues, such as labels, color-coded systems, and visible calendars, can help your husband remember tasks and appointments. Consider using visual aids for routines and to-do lists.

d. Minimize Distractions: Identify potential distractions in the home and work together to minimize them. For example, create a quiet workspace away from high-traffic areas and limit the presence of electronic devices during focused activities.

e. Implement Storage Solutions: Having adequate storage solutions can help keep belongings organized and easily accessible. Use storage bins, shelves, and cabinets to keep items in their designated places.

f. Maintain a Daily Tidy-Up Routine: Encourage daily tidying up to keep the home organized. This can be a shared responsibility between you and your husband, making it a part of your routine.

Creating Routines and Schedules

Routines and schedules provide structure and predictability, which can be particularly beneficial for individuals with ADHD. Consistent routines help manage time, reduce stress, and improve overall functioning.

a. Establish a Morning and Evening Routine: Create morning and evening routines to start and end the day on a positive and organized note. This can include activities such as setting out clothes, preparing meals, and reviewing the next day's schedule.

b. Use Timers and Alarms: Timers and alarms can be valuable tools for time management. Set reminders for important tasks and activities to help your husband stay on track throughout the day.

c. Prioritize Tasks: Encourage your husband to prioritize tasks based on importance and deadlines.

Breaking tasks down into manageable steps and tackling them one at a time can reduce feelings of overwhelm.

d. Include Breaks and Relaxation Time: Include regular rest periods and breaks in the schedule. By taking breaks, you can maintain focus and avoid burnout.

e. Be Flexible: While routines are essential, it's crucial to be flexible and adjust them as needed. Life can be unpredictable, and being adaptable can reduce frustration when unexpected events occur.

f. Involve Your Husband in Planning: To make sure the routines and timetables suit his tastes and demands, involve your husband in the planning process. Collaboration creates a sense of accountability and ownership.

Seek Outside Support

Living with an ADHD husband can be challenging, and seeking outside support can be beneficial for both of you.

a. Educate Family Members and Friends: Educate family members and friends about ADHD to increase their understanding and support. This can foster a more compassionate and inclusive environment for your husband.

b. Consider Therapy or Support Groups: Individual or couples therapy can provide a safe space to address challenges and develop coping strategies. Additionally, joining support groups for individuals with ADHD and their partners can offer valuable insights and shared experiences.

c. Professional Organizational Help: If organizing the home feels overwhelming, consider enlisting the help of a professional organizer to develop systems tailored to your family's needs.

Encouraging Self-Care and Stress Management

Living with an ADHD husband can be demanding, and it's essential to prioritize self-care and stress management for both partners. Taking care of oneself enables better support and understanding within the relationship. In this chapter, we will explore the importance of self-care and stress management for you and your ADHD husband, along with practical strategies to promote well-being.

1. Recognize the Importance of Self-Care:
Self-care involves intentionally taking time for activities that nourish your physical, emotional, and mental well-being. It is not selfish but rather a necessary practice to maintain balance and prevent

burnout. Encourage your husband to embrace self-care and engage in activities he enjoys. These could include hobbies, spending time with friends, exercising, or simply having quiet moments for relaxation.

2. Prioritize Sleep: Sleep plays a vital role in managing ADHD symptoms and overall health. Encourage your husband to establish a regular sleep routine and aim for consistent bedtimes and wake-up times. Create a calming bedtime routine, such as reading a book or practicing relaxation techniques, to help him unwind before sleep.

3. Manage Stress: Stress can exacerbate ADHD symptoms and impact emotional well-being. Encourage your husband to identify sources of stress and explore coping mechanisms to manage it effectively. Engaging in mindfulness practices, such as meditation or yoga, can be beneficial in reducing stress and increasing focus and emotional regulation.

4. Set Boundaries and Practice Assertiveness: Setting boundaries is crucial for both partners in a relationship. Encourage open communication about each other's needs and limitations, and be assertive in expressing your boundaries. By respecting each other's boundaries, you can prevent unnecessary conflict and create a supportive environment for self-care and stress management.

5. Promote Healthy Eating Habits: A balanced diet can positively influence cognitive function and mood. Encourage your husband to maintain a nutritious diet with regular meals and snacks. Limiting sugary and processed foods can also help manage fluctuations in energy and mood.

6. Engage in Physical Activity Together: Physical activity benefits both partners' well-being and can be a fun way to spend time together. Consider engaging in exercises you both enjoy, such as walking, dancing, or biking. Exercising together fosters emotional connection and mutual support while reaping the benefits of increased physical activity.

7. Create a Relaxing Environment: A calming and organized living space can contribute to stress reduction. Work together to create an environment that promotes relaxation and comfort. Include elements such as soothing colors, soft lighting, and comfortable furniture to make your home a sanctuary.

8. Practice Mindfulness as a Couple: Incorporate mindfulness practices as a couple to deepen emotional connection and understanding. Participate in mindfulness exercises, such as mindful breathing or guided meditation, together. Mindfulness can help you both manage stress and improve communication by staying present in your interactions.

Chapter Four

Managing ADHD in Daily Life

Living with ADHD requires developing effective strategies to manage its symptoms and navigate daily challenges. In this chapter, we will explore coping mechanisms for forgetfulness and disorganization, as well as techniques to address procrastination and improve time management.

Coping with Forgetfulness and Disorganization

Forgetfulness and disorganization are common symptoms of ADHD that can impact daily life. Implementing practical strategies can help individuals with ADHD and their partners cope with these challenges.

a. Use Visual Reminders: Visual aids, such as sticky notes, whiteboards, or phone reminders, can serve as helpful cues to remember tasks and appointments. Placing these reminders in prominent locations can increase their effectiveness.

b. Create Checklists: Creating checklists for daily tasks and routines can help organize thoughts and ensure important tasks are not overlooked. Encourage your partner to check off items as they are completed, providing a sense of accomplishment.

c. Establish a Centralized Calendar: Maintain a centralized calendar for all family events, appointments, and deadlines. Sharing this calendar with your partner can ensure that both of you are aware of upcoming commitments.

d. Use Technology: Embrace technology to stay organized. Digital calendars, task management apps, and note-taking tools can help individuals with ADHD keep track of important information and events.

e. Develop Organizational Systems: Work together to develop organizational systems for the home. Use designated storage spaces for essential items, and create routines for organizing belongings regularly.

f. Reduce Clutter: A clutter-free environment can lessen distractions and make it easier to locate items. Encourage regular decluttering sessions and discourage holding onto unnecessary items.

Dealing with Procrastination and Time Management Challenges

Procrastination and time management issues can lead to increased stress and incomplete tasks. Employing effective techniques can help individuals with ADHD and their partners address these challenges.

a. Break Tasks into Smaller Steps: For people with ADHD, big chores can be daunting and cause delays. It may feel more feasible to complete projects if you divide them into smaller, more manageable phases.

b. Use Time Blocking: Implement time blocking techniques to allocate specific time slots for different tasks and activities. This can help create structure and ensure that essential tasks are addressed.

c. Set Realistic Deadlines: Encourage setting realistic deadlines for tasks and projects. Be understanding if your partner needs additional time to complete tasks due to ADHD-related challenges.

d. Use External Cues: External cues, such as timers or alarms, can help individuals with ADHD stay on track and manage time effectively. Set reminders for breaks, task transitions, and appointments.

e. Prioritize Tasks: Help your partner prioritize tasks based on urgency and importance. Focus on completing high-priority tasks first, reducing the risk of procrastination on critical responsibilities.

f. Reward Positive Behavior: Positive reinforcement can be a powerful motivator for individuals with ADHD. Offer rewards or incentives for completing tasks or adhering to time management strategies.

g. Limit Distractions: Create a distraction-free environment during focused tasks. Minimize noise, turn off electronic devices, and establish a dedicated workspace to improve concentration.

h. Practice the Two-Minute Rule: Encourage your partner to tackle small tasks that take two minutes or less immediately. This can prevent these tasks from piling up and becoming overwhelming.

By implementing coping strategies for forgetfulness and disorganization, as well as techniques to address procrastination and improve time management, individuals with ADHD and their partners can enhance daily life and reduce stress. Recognize that managing ADHD is an ongoing process, and support each other in developing effective strategies that work best for your unique circumstances.

Helping Your Husband Stay on Task and Complete Projects

Helping your husband stay on task and complete projects is an essential aspect of supporting him in managing his ADHD symptoms effectively. ADHD can lead to difficulties with focus, time management, and organization, making it challenging to complete tasks and projects. In this section, we will explore strategies to assist your husband in staying on track and accomplishing his goals.

1. Set Clear Goals and Prioritize Tasks: Work together with your husband to set clear goals for projects and daily tasks. Break down larger projects into smaller, manageable steps, and prioritize them based on importance and deadlines. Having a clear roadmap can provide direction and reduce overwhelm.

2. Create a Structured Environment: Establish a structured environment that fosters productivity and minimizes distractions. Designate a dedicated workspace for your husband to work on tasks and projects. Keep this area organized and free from clutter to promote focus.

3. Use Visual and Auditory Cues: Visual and auditory cues can be helpful reminders to stay on task. Utilize timers, alarms, or phone notifications to signal the start and end of focused work sessions. Visual cues, such as checklists or progress charts, can provide a sense of accomplishment as tasks are completed.

4. Offer Gentle Reminders: Be supportive in offering gentle reminders when you notice your husband getting off track. Avoid being critical or impatient, and instead, provide encouragement and positive reinforcement for his efforts.

5. Practice Task Chunking: Task chunking involves breaking tasks into smaller, more manageable chunks. Encourage your husband to work on one chunk at a time, celebrating each completion as a milestone toward project completion.

6. Provide Accountability: Offer to be an accountability partner for your husband. Regularly check in on his progress, discuss goals, and celebrate achievements together. Knowing that someone is cheering him on can be a powerful motivator.

7. Use Rewards and Incentives: Implement a reward system for accomplishing tasks and completing projects. Offer small rewards or incentives for meeting specific milestones. Positive reinforcement can increase motivation and boost confidence.

8. Support Time Management Techniques: Encourage your husband to use time management techniques such as time blocking, prioritization, and setting realistic deadlines. These techniques can help him manage his time effectively and prevent tasks from piling up.

9. Be Patient and Understanding: Living with ADHD can be challenging, and your husband may face setbacks along the way. Be patient and understanding, offering a safe space for him to share his feelings and frustrations.

Remember that helping your husband stay on task and complete projects requires empathy, patience, and open communication. Working together as a team, you can support his efforts and celebrate his achievements, leading to a more fulfilling and productive life despite the challenges of ADHD.

Chapter Five

Strengthening Emotional Connection

Maintaining a strong emotional connection is vital for any relationship, and it holds particular significance when one partner has ADHD. In this chapter, we will explore strategies to nurture emotional intimacy and navigate emotional sensitivity to enhance the bond between you and your ADHD husband.

Nurturing Emotional Intimacy

A strong and satisfying relationship is built on emotional connection. It entails being honest, open, and accepting of one another's sentiments and emotions. Following are some ideas for fostering emotional closeness with your ADHD husband:

a. Create Quality Time Together: Make an effort to spend quality time together regularly. Engage in activities that you both enjoy, such as hobbies, date nights, or simply talking and connecting on a deeper level.

b. Practice Active Listening: Show genuine interest in what your husband has to say. Practice active listening by giving your full attention, maintaining eye contact, and offering validating responses.

c. Share Your Feelings: Be open and honest about your emotions and thoughts. Share your joys, fears, and concerns with your husband, encouraging him to do the same.

d. Offer Emotional Support: Be a source of emotional support for your husband. Be understanding and empathetic when he faces challenges related to ADHD, and celebrate his successes and achievements.

e. Communicate with Kindness: Choose your words and tone carefully during discussions to avoid triggering emotional sensitivity. Communicate with kindness and respect, promoting a safe and nurturing environment for emotional expression.

f. Be Patient and Non-Judgmental: Living with ADHD can bring moments of frustration or impulsivity. Practice patience and non-judgment when your husband faces difficulties, and remember that mistakes are opportunities for growth and learning.

g. Engage in Physical Affection: Physical affection, such as hugging, holding hands, and cuddling, can strengthen emotional connection and foster feelings of comfort and security.

Handling Emotional Sensitivity

Individuals with ADHD may experience emotional sensitivity, which can impact their reactions to different situations. Understanding and managing emotional sensitivity is crucial for promoting a harmonious and supportive relationship. Here are strategies to handle emotional sensitivity:

a. Identify Triggers: Together, identify emotional triggers that can lead to heightened sensitivity. Understanding these triggers can help you both navigate potential challenges more effectively.

b. Allow Emotional Space: If your husband becomes emotionally sensitive, allow him the space he needs to process his feelings. Avoid pushing for immediate explanations and give him time to collect his thoughts.

c. Offer Reassurance: During moments of emotional sensitivity, offer reassurance and comfort. Let your husband know that you are there for him and that his emotions are valid and respected.

d. Encourage Emotional Regulation Techniques: Help your husband develop emotional regulation techniques, such as deep breathing exercises or mindfulness practices. These tools can assist him in managing intense emotions.

e. Avoid Blaming or Criticizing: Avoid blaming or criticizing your partner in tense moments. Instead, emphasize using constructive communication to work together to discover answers.

f. Seek Support Together: Consider attending couples counseling or therapy to address emotional sensitivity as a team. A professional can provide guidance and techniques to enhance emotional communication and understanding.

g. Set Boundaries for Conflict Resolution: Establish boundaries for how conflicts are resolved to ensure that emotions are managed respectfully. Avoid engaging in heated arguments and agree on taking breaks when needed.

h. Celebrate Emotional Vulnerability: Encourage emotional vulnerability in your relationship. Celebrate and appreciate each other's willingness to share feelings, fostering a deeper emotional connection.

Balancing Emotional Needs in the Relationship

Balancing emotional needs in a relationship is essential for fostering a strong and healthy bond between partners. When one partner has ADHD, it can add a layer of complexity to meeting each other's emotional needs effectively. Here are some strategies to achieve a balanced emotional connection in a relationship where one partner has ADHD:

1. Communicate Openly and Honestly: Establish a safe space for open and honest communication. Encourage each other to express feelings, concerns, and needs without fear of judgment. Active listening and empathy are crucial during these conversations.

2. Understand ADHD's Impact on Emotions: Educate yourselves about ADHD and its effects on emotions. Understanding how ADHD influences emotions can lead to greater compassion and patience, enabling both partners to navigate emotional challenges with empathy.

3. Find Compromise: Seek compromises that address both partners' emotional needs. It's essential to find a middle ground where both of you feel valued and supported.

4. Set Realistic Expectations: Recognize that neither partner is perfect, and setting unrealistic expectations can lead to disappointment and frustration. Understand that managing emotions in a relationship with ADHD requires understanding and flexibility.

5. Offer Support and Encouragement: Be each other's support system. Offer encouragement during challenging times and celebrate each other's successes and achievements. Being supportive can strengthen emotional connection and boost each other's confidence.

6. Establish Boundaries: Establish clear boundaries to ensure that both partners have time and space to tend to their emotional well-being. Respecting each other's need for personal time can promote a healthy balance in the relationship.

7. Manage Stress Together: Work as a team to manage stress in the relationship. Find healthy coping mechanisms, such as mindfulness practices or physical activities, to alleviate stress and create a more harmonious atmosphere.

8. Practice Empathy and Emotional Validation: Be empathetic and validate each other's emotions. Let your partner know that their feelings are acknowledged and respected, even if you may not fully understand their experience.

9. Spend Quality Time Together: Make time for quality moments together to nurture emotional intimacy. Engage in activities that bring joy and strengthen your emotional connection.

Remember that balancing emotional needs in a relationship is an ongoing process that requires continuous effort and understanding from both partners. By creating an environment of open communication, empathy, and support, you can strengthen emotional connection and cultivate a loving and fulfilling relationship, even amidst the challenges of ADHD.

Chapter Six

Handling Impulsivity and Hyperactivity

Living with ADHD often involves coping with impulsivity and hyperactivity, which can present unique challenges in daily life. In this chapter, we will explore the impact of impulsivity and strategies for managing hyperactivity to create a supportive environment for both partners in the relationship.

Understanding Impulsivity and Its Impact

Impulsivity is a hallmark symptom of ADHD and refers to the tendency to act without thinking about the consequences. It can manifest in impulsive decisions, interrupting others, and difficulty delaying gratification. Understanding the impact of impulsivity is essential for both partners to navigate its effects on the relationship:

1. Recognizing Impulsive Behaviors: Be aware of impulsive behaviors displayed by your ADHD husband. These behaviors may include impulsive spending, making hasty decisions, or being easily distracted during conversations.

2. Communicate Calmly: When impulsive behaviors arise, communicate calmly and non-judgmentally. Avoid reacting emotionally and instead, seek to understand the underlying reasons for the impulsivity.

3. Encourage Self-Reflection: Encourage your husband to practice self-reflection and identify triggers for impulsive behavior. By recognizing patterns, he can develop strategies to manage impulsivity more effectively.

4. Implement Delaying Tactics: Encourage your husband to use delaying tactics when faced with impulsive decisions. Taking a moment to pause and consider the consequences can help reduce impulsive actions.

5. Establish Rules for Major Decisions: Establish guidelines for making significant decisions together. This can provide a framework for considering options and evaluating potential outcomes, reducing impulsive choices.

6. Seek Support and Guidance: If your husband's impulsivity negatively affects his life or your marriage, you might want to think about getting help from a therapist or counselor with experience treating ADHD. Professional advice can provide insightful tips and proactive methods for controlling impulsivity.

Strategies for Managing Hyperactivity

Hyperactivity is another core symptom of ADHD and involves excessive restlessness, fidgeting, and difficulty remaining still. Managing hyperactivity is essential for creating a calm and productive environment:

1. Engage in Physical Activity: Encourage your husband to engage in regular physical activity to release excess energy. Exercise can help reduce hyperactivity and improve focus.

2. Create Structured Routines: Establish structured daily routines that include designated periods for focused activities and relaxation. Consistent routines can help manage hyperactivity and create predictability.

3. Provide Sensory Outlets: Offer sensory outlets, such as stress balls or fidget toys, to help your husband channel excess energy in a non-disruptive manner.

4. Use Time Blocking: Implement time-blocking techniques to allocate specific time slots for focused tasks and physical activity. This can provide a balance between periods of activity and periods of calm.

5. Encourage Mindful Practices: Practicing mindfulness and deep-breathing exercises can help your husband manage hyperactivity and stay present in the moment.

6. Minimize Environmental Triggers: Identify and minimize environmental triggers that may exacerbate hyperactivity, such as excessive noise or clutter.

7. Set Realistic Expectations: Understand that hyperactivity is a symptom of ADHD and be patient with your husband. Set realistic expectations for completing tasks, recognizing that breaks and movement breaks may be necessary.

8. Utilize Breaks Effectively: Encourage your husband to take short breaks during tasks that require sustained focus. Short breaks can provide an opportunity to release excess energy and return to the task with renewed focus.

9. Create a Calm Environment: Establish a calm and organized home environment to reduce sensory overload and promote relaxation.

10. Reward Focus and Calmness: Provide positive reinforcement for moments of focus and calmness. Acknowledging these behaviors can encourage their recurrence.

By understanding impulsivity's impact and implementing strategies to manage hyperactivity, couples can create a supportive and understanding environment that enables both partners to thrive.

Remember that managing impulsivity and hyperactivity is a shared responsibility, and open communication and patience are vital to navigating these symptoms successfully in the relationship.

Supporting Your Husband in Social Situations

Supporting your husband in social situations is essential for helping him navigate the challenges that may arise due to ADHD. Social interactions can be overwhelming for individuals with ADHD, but with understanding and support, you can create a more comfortable and enjoyable experience for both of you. Here are some strategies to support your husband in social situations:

1. Prioritize Communication: Before attending social events, communicate with your husband about what to expect, who will be present, and the general flow of the gathering. Providing this information in advance can reduce anxiety and uncertainty.

2. Prepare for Small Talk: Help your husband prepare for a small talk by brainstorming conversation starters and topics he can use in social settings. These prompts can give him a sense of confidence when engaging with others.

3. Offer Emotional Support: In social situations, your husband may feel overwhelmed or anxious. Offer emotional support by staying by his side, providing reassurance, and being understanding if he needs to take breaks.

4. Create a Signal: Create a discrete cue that your husband can use to convey when he needs to regroup or step away from social encounters. By doing this, embarrassing or uncomfortable situations may be avoided.

5. Encourage Active Listening: Encourage your husband to practice active listening in social interactions. Remind him to focus on the speaker, maintain eye contact, and ask questions to stay engaged in conversations.

6. Respect Boundaries: Understand and respect your husband's need for personal space and time alone. Social situations can be draining for individuals with ADHD, and they may require downtime to recharge.

7. Practice Nonverbal Cues: In social situations with larger groups, it can be challenging for your husband to keep up with multiple conversations. Use nonverbal cues, such as a gentle touch or glance, to indicate when he may want to participate in a different conversation.

8. Encourage Socializing in Smaller Groups: Smaller group settings may be more manageable for your husband. Encourage opportunities for one-on-one or smaller group interactions to reduce potential overwhelm.

9. Focus on Quality Over Quantity: Instead of attending numerous social events, prioritize quality interactions. Choose social gatherings that are meaningful and align with your husband's interests to make the experience more enjoyable.

10. Be Patient and Understanding: Be patient and understanding if your husband feels anxious or struggles with social interactions. Offer encouragement and remind him that it's okay to take things at his own pace.

Chapter Seven

Managing ADHD-Related Challenges in Intimacy

Intimacy is a vital aspect of any romantic relationship, but managing ADHD-related challenges can present unique complexities. In this chapter, we will explore strategies to address sexual intimacy and overcome relationship stressors related to ADHD.

Addressing Sexual Intimacy and ADHD

ADHD can impact sexual intimacy in various ways, from difficulties with focus and distraction to impulsivity and emotional sensitivity. Here are some strategies to address sexual intimacy in the context of ADHD:

1. Open Communication: Establish open and honest communication about sexual desires, needs, and concerns. Discussing sexual intimacy in a non-judgmental and understanding manner can foster a deeper emotional connection and a sense of safety in the relationship.

2. Set the Mood: Create a relaxing and distraction-free environment for sexual encounters. Dim the lights, eliminate potential interruptions, and engage in activities that promote emotional closeness before engaging in sexual intimacy.

3. Practice Mindfulness: Incorporate mindfulness practices into sexual experiences to help your partner stay present and focused. Encourage him to focus on physical sensations and emotional connection during intimate moments.

4. Be Patient and Understanding: Be patient and understanding if your partner experiences challenges related to sexual intimacy due to ADHD symptoms. Avoid placing undue pressure on him, and instead, foster an environment of support and empathy.

5. Experiment with Timing: Experiment with different times of the day for sexual intimacy to find when your partner feels most focused and relaxed. Timing can play a significant role in enhancing the experience for both partners.

6. Explore Sensate Focus: Sensate focus exercises involve focusing on physical sensations rather than performance or achieving specific outcomes. Engaging in sensate focus exercises can help reduce performance anxiety and increase emotional connection.

7. Seek Professional Guidance: If sexual intimacy challenges persist and impact your relationship, consider seeking guidance from a sex therapist or counselor experienced in working with couples dealing with ADHD-related intimacy issues.

Overcoming Relationship Stressors

ADHD-related challenges can contribute to relationship stressors that may strain the emotional connection between partners. Here are strategies to overcome these stressors and strengthen the relationship:

1. Cultivate Empathy and Understanding: Practice empathy and understanding when your partner faces challenges due to ADHD. Recognize that ADHD can affect various aspects of life, and offering support and compassion can enhance the emotional bond between you.

2. Manage Anger and Frustration: Coping with ADHD-related challenges may lead to moments of anger and frustration. Learn healthy ways to manage these emotions and engage in constructive communication during conflicts.

3. Divide Responsibilities Fairly: Dividing household responsibilities fairly can reduce stress and prevent feelings of resentment. Understand each other's strengths and limitations and create a balanced distribution of tasks.

4. Schedule Regular Check-Ins: Schedule regular check-ins to discuss how each partner is feeling in the relationship. Use these discussions as opportunities to express needs, address concerns, and reinforce emotional connection.

5. Set Boundaries: Establish clear boundaries to prevent overwhelm and burnout. Respect each other's personal space and the need for downtime to recharge emotionally.

6. Practice Gratitude: Cultivate gratitude in your relationship by acknowledging and appreciating each other's efforts and contributions. Expressing gratitude can foster a positive and loving atmosphere.

7. Seek Support Together: Consider seeking support together from a couples therapist or counselor. Professional guidance can offer insights and tools to manage relationship stressors and improve communication.

8. Make Time for Each Other: Prioritize quality time together to nurture emotional intimacy. Engage in activities that you both enjoy and strengthen your connection.

9. Plan Fun and Relaxing Activities: Plan fun and relaxing activities to reduce stress and promote bonding. Engaging in enjoyable experiences together can strengthen the emotional connection.

Seeking Professional Help When Needed

Seeking professional help when needed is a crucial step in managing the challenges of living with ADHD and maintaining a healthy relationship. Professional guidance can provide valuable insights, strategies, and support to navigate the complexities of ADHD-related issues effectively. Here are some reasons why seeking professional help is essential:

1. Expertise and Experience: Mental health professionals, therapists, and counselors have expertise and experience in working with individuals and couples dealing with ADHD-related challenges. They can offer personalized strategies and interventions tailored to your unique circumstances.

2. Non-Judgmental Environment: Therapy sessions provide a safe and non-judgmental space to discuss concerns, emotions, and relationship dynamics. It allows partners to express themselves openly and work towards solutions without fear of criticism.

3. Communication Improvement: A therapist can facilitate open and constructive communication between partners, helping to address conflicts and misunderstandings effectively.

4. Skill Development: Therapy can focus on skill development, such as time management, coping strategies, and emotional regulation, which are essential in managing ADHD-related challenges.

5. Validation and Support: Seeking professional help can offer validation and support for both partners. It acknowledges that living with ADHD can be challenging and that seeking help is a proactive step toward creating a healthier and more fulfilling relationship.

6. Long-Term Benefits: Investing in professional help can have long-term benefits for the relationship and both partners' emotional well-being. It equips couples with tools to navigate challenges and fosters resilience in facing future obstacles.

Remember that seeking professional help is not a sign of weakness but rather a proactive decision to enhance the quality of your relationship and individual lives. Whether attending couples counseling, seeking individual therapy, or engaging in ADHD-specific support groups, professional assistance can be a transformative step towards creating a more harmonious and loving partnership.

Chapter Eight

Self-Care for the Partner of an ADHD Individual

Being in a relationship with someone who has ADHD can be both rewarding and challenging. As the partner of an individual with ADHD, it's essential to prioritize self-care to maintain your emotional well-being and support your partner effectively. In this chapter, we will explore self-care strategies for partners of individuals with ADHD, including recognizing your needs and emotions and seeking personal support and community.

Recognizing Your Needs and Emotions

Being in a relationship with someone with ADHD can bring unique stressors and emotions. It's essential to recognize your own needs and emotions to address them effectively. Here are some self-care strategies to help you navigate your feelings and prioritize your well-being:

1. Self-Reflection: Take time for self-reflection to understand your feelings and reactions to specific situations in the relationship. Identifying your emotions can help you communicate more effectively with your partner and seek appropriate support.

2. Validate Your Emotions: Recognize that it is normal to experience a range of emotions, including frustration, stress, and even occasional resentment. Validating your emotions allows you to process them healthily.

3. Set Boundaries: Set up distinct limits to safeguard your well-being. Setting aside time for leisure and participating in enjoyable activities are examples of boundaries.

4. Prioritize Self-Care Activities: Engage in self-care activities that promote relaxation and emotional well-being. This can include exercise, mindfulness practices, hobbies, or spending time with supportive friends and family.

5. Practice Gratitude: Cultivate gratitude by focusing on the positive aspects of your relationship and the strengths of your partner. Expressing gratitude can enhance your emotional connection and foster a positive outlook.

6. Seek Moments of Solitude: Schedule moments of solitude to recharge emotionally. Taking time alone can provide a sense of balance and reduce overwhelm.

7. Communicate Your Needs: Openly communicate your needs and feelings to your partner. Sharing your emotions can foster a deeper emotional connection and allow your partner to understand how they can support you.

8. Limit Stressful Triggers: Be mindful of situations or environments that may increase stress. Reducing exposure to stressful triggers can positively impact your emotional well-being.

Seeking Personal Support and Community

Having a support system is crucial for partners of individuals with ADHD. Connecting with others who understand your experiences can provide validation, insight, and encouragement. Here are ways to seek personal support and find community:

1. Join Support Groups: Look for local or online support groups specifically designed for partners of individuals with ADHD. These groups can provide a safe space to share experiences, exchange advice, and gain emotional support.

2. Attend Couples Counseling: Consider attending couples counseling to address challenges and improve communication in the relationship. A therapist experienced in working with ADHD-related issues can provide valuable guidance and support.

3. Talk to Friends and Family: Reach out to friends and family members you trust to talk about your experiences and feelings. Having a supportive network can be reassuring and provide valuable perspectives.

4. Engage in Individual Therapy: Individual therapy can offer a private space to discuss your emotions and concerns with a mental health professional. A therapist can help you develop coping strategies and promote self-awareness.

5. Participate in ADHD Workshops: Attend workshops or seminars focused on ADHD and relationships. Learning more about ADHD can lead to greater understanding and empathy for your partner's experiences.

7. Seek Online Resources: Explore reputable online resources that provide information, tips, and support for partners of individuals with ADHD.

8. Participate in Relaxing Activities Together: Engage in relaxing activities with your partner to foster emotional connection and create positive experiences.

Remember that seeking personal support and connecting with others can enhance your emotional well-being and strengthen your ability to support your partner. By recognizing your needs and emotions and seeking support, you can maintain a balanced and fulfilling relationship, even amidst the challenges of living with ADHD. Prioritizing self-care allows you to show up as the best version of yourself for both your partner and yourself.

Practicing Patience and Resilience in the Relationship

Practicing patience and resilience in a relationship where one partner has ADHD is essential for nurturing a strong and enduring bond. Living with ADHD can present daily challenges that may test the patience of both partners. By cultivating patience and resilience, couples can navigate these obstacles with greater understanding and empathy. Here are some strategies to practice patience and resilience in the relationship:

1. Educate Yourself about ADHD: Understanding the nature of ADHD, its symptoms, and its impact on daily life can foster empathy and patience. Educate yourself about ADHD through books, articles, and reliable online resources.

2. Communicate Openly and Honestly: Establish open and honest communication about the challenges posed by ADHD. Share your feelings and concerns, and be receptive to your partner's experiences and emotions.

3. Avoid Blame and Judgment: Instead of blaming your partner or yourself for ADHD-related difficulties, focus on finding solutions together. Avoid criticizing each other and seek to understand the underlying reasons behind certain behaviors.

5. Cultivate Emotional Regulation: Practice emotional regulation techniques to manage frustration or impatience during challenging moments. Deep breathing or taking a short break can help you respond with patience instead of reacting impulsively.

6. Set Realistic Expectations: Set realistic expectations for both yourself and your partner.

Understand that managing ADHD involves ongoing effort and progress may come in small increments.

7. Use Humor as a Coping Mechanism: Use humor to diffuse tense situations and foster a lighthearted atmosphere. Laughing together can strengthen your bond and reduce stress.

8. Embrace a Team Approach: Approach challenges as a team, collaborating to find solutions and supporting each other throughout the process. The sense of unity can boost resilience and strengthen the relationship.

10. Practice Self-Compassion: Be compassionate towards yourself and your partner. Acknowledge that no one is perfect, and it's normal to face difficulties in any relationship. Treat yourselves with kindness and understanding.

Practicing patience and resilience is an ongoing process that requires commitment and understanding from both partners. By approaching ADHD-related challenges with patience, open communication, and a sense of teamwork, couples can foster a supportive and loving relationship. Remember that building resilience together allows you to overcome obstacles and grow stronger as a couple, deepening your emotional connection and creating a lasting bond.

Exclusive bonus

20 ADHD-friendly activities for couples that can help foster connection, enjoyment, and understanding

1. **Nature Walks:** Exploring a park or nature trail provides sensory stimulation and a calm environment for meaningful conversations.

2. **Cooking Together:** Collaborating on a meal allows for creativity, teamwork, and a shared sense of accomplishment.

3. **Art Night:** Engage in creative activities like painting, drawing, or crafting to express yourselves and unwind.

4. **Board Games:** Opt for games that require strategic thinking and quick decision-making to keep both partners engaged.

5. **Outdoor Sports:** Activities like biking, frisbee, or tennis provide a physical outlet and a way to channel excess energy.

6. **Movie or TV Show Marathon:** Choose a series or movies you both enjoy, creating a relaxed bonding experience.

7. **Visit a Museum or Art Gallery:** Explore local culture while focusing on the exhibits that catch your interest.

8. **Picnic at the Park:** Pack a lunch and enjoy each other's company in a pleasant outdoor setting.

9. **DIY Projects:** Collaborate on home improvement tasks, fostering teamwork and a sense of accomplishment.

10. **Mindfulness Meditation:** Practice mindfulness together to improve focus, reduce stress, and deepen your connection.

11. **Karaoke Night:** Singing along to favorite tunes is a fun way to let loose and enjoy each other's company.

12. **Attend a Workshop:** Join a class or workshop to learn something new together, like cooking, dancing, or photography.

13. **Trivia Night:** Participate in trivia games that challenge your knowledge and quick thinking.

14. **Volunteer Together:** Engaging in volunteer work can strengthen your bond while giving back to the community.

15. **Visit a Zoo or Aquarium:** Observe animals and marine life, sparking interesting conversations.

16. **Build a Puzzle:** Engage in a puzzle-solving activity that encourages focus and collaboration.

17. **Take a Day Trip:** Explore a nearby town, go for a scenic drive, or visit a local landmark.

18. **Stargazing:** Spend an evening looking at the stars, contemplating the universe, and enjoying quiet moments together.

19. **Dance Night:** Put on some music and have a dance party at home, encouraging movement and fun.

20. **Yoga or Tai Chi:** Practice calming, centering activities that can help manage stress and increase mindfulness.

Remember, the key is to choose activities that both partners enjoy and that allow for flexibility and adaptability. By engaging in these activities together, you can create shared experiences that accommodate the unique aspects of ADHD while enhancing your relationship.

"We must accept finite disappointment, but never lose infinite hope." — Martin Luther King, Jr.

Dear Reader,

Thank you for choosing to read my book, **HOW TO LIVE WITH AN ADHD HUSBAND**. I hope you found it informative and helpful. If you have a moment, I would greatly appreciate it if you could leave a review on Amazon. Your feedback would help me better understand what readers appreciate about my work, and would also provide valuable information to potential readers.

Your honest review would be greatly appreciated, and would help me continue to improve as a writer. I truly value your opinion, and I thank you in advance for taking the time to share your thoughts. Thank you again for choosing to read my book, and for considering leaving a review.

Best regards,

Dr Micheal Wilson.

Printed in Great Britain
by Amazon

40986632R00056